ON EAGLE'S WINGS

Poems About God's Miraculous Power

ON EAGLE'S WINGS

Sharon Burrell

On Eagle's Wings: Poems About God's Miraculous Power
Copyright © 2024, by Sharon Burrell

ISBN: 979-8-218-53327-4

Published by: Kingdom Training and Consulting, LLC.
Printed in the United States of America

Author Photos: Lisa Burrell
Internal Layout and Design: InSCRIBEd Inspiration, LLC.
Edited by: Sharon Burrell, Penda L. James, Lisa Burrell, Tracy Fagan
Cover Art: InSCRIBEd Inspiration, LLC.

All rights reserved. No part of this book may be reproduced or transmitted in any form electronic, or mechanical, including photocopying and recording, or held in any information storage and retrieval system without permission in writing from the author and publisher.

DEDICATION

To my husband **Rodney**.

To our children and grandchildren:
LaTrese and her husband **Donnie**
    (**Christine** our angel and **Paris**)
Brandi and her husband **Demond**
    (**Destiny, Daniella, Demi, Dallas, Danica, Della**)
Rodney and his wife **Lisa**
    (**Niko, Roman**)
Joel and his wife **Jessica**
    (**Elijah, Selah**)
Christopher and his wife **Fabiana**
    (**Nicholas, Marco**)
Joy
    (**Kira**)
Christa

For my sister, Dawn Yvette.

LORD, I THANK YOU

For getting me up this morning
And starting me truly on my way
I thank you for my health and healing
I thank you for my sight
I thank you that I'm able to move

Thank you, Thank you, Thank you
For each of the seven precious lives
You loaned to me and trusted
That a mother I WOULD BE
For my children for their lives
Being dedicated to YOU
For YOUR PURPOSE
Being fulfilled in each of their lives
For the lives of my grandchildren and
For DIVINE PROTECTION FROM YOU

8-8-2015

ACKNOWLEDGMENTS

My Heavenly Father, Jesus Christ and the **Holy Spirit** for leading and guiding me through this process.

I am grateful for the time and love that **Penda L. James** and the Ink Spill writing group. I'm grateful that she was led to shed light, love and purpose to us all. Ms. James stepped up and helped me to take hold of my purpose.

Pastor Tracy Fagan of Kingdom Publishing was a light in a dark place encouraging me to write and share the things that GOD placed within my Spirit.

Pastors Alexander and Loretta Gordon, both who have gone home to be with the Lord but acted as spiritual parents, encouraged and supported me during my spiritual journey.

ALL those who have contributed to my life to support and help me grow.

CONTENTS

Vision **1**
    An Empty Cross 5
    Be What God Wants 7
    I Want To Go To Heaven 8
    Show Your Love 10
    Vision 11
    Do You See 12
    Forgiveness 14

Healing **17**
    Mending A Shattered Heart 21
    In His Hands 22
    A New Creature 23
    Do We Know 26
    Total Acceptance 27
    Understanding Being Alone 29
    Why Do We 31
    Healing 33
    God's Love Is Special 34
    I Am A Miracle 35

Purpose 37
   A Dreamer 41
   If I Could Be A Flower 43
   Breathing 44
   Be What God Desires 45
   Freedom 46
   Don't Lean On The Arm Of Flesh 47
   The Challenge Of Life 48
   Finding My Way Home 49
   Praying Grandma 51
   Forget Yesterday 53
   Affirmation 54
   How Great Thou Art 56
   Entertaining Angels Unaware 59

VISION
The Eagle's Eyesight

Did you know the eagle is the only bird that sees a storm coming miles before it actually arrives? It will turn to face the storm, stretch out and lock its wings and fly directly into it. The wind will carry the eagle above the storm.

According to traditional American Indian beliefs, the Creator made all the birds of the sky when the World was new. God equipped the eagle with exceptionally sharp vision of the eye structure like no others. **Each eye has two foveae - areas of acute vision** - as compared with the human eye which only has one. The cones in the eagle's fovea are very small and tightly grouped, allowing the eagle to see small details from extreme distances. The eyesight of an eagle eye is estimated to be four to eight times stronger than that of the average human. It is among the sharpest in the animal kingdom. They can view colors at four times the intensity of the human eye.

Eagles catch and eat live rabbits, mice, fish, and small game daily. This is where their vision is crucial since they hunt from the air. I believe God wants us to soar as eagles and exhibit their characteristics of **truth, majesty, strength, courage, wisdom, power and freedom**.

You can look for the storms in advance and be fearless; face storms head on and let the wind of our Heavenly Father carry you under His wings above the clouds.

GOD allows prophets and prophetesses to dream dreams and to experience visions. They say the eyes are the windows to the soul for those who are looking for it. If you are looking out, it is imperative to tap into the vision that God has provided to guide you through life's storms and challenges to victory.

AN EMPTY CROSS

An empty cross
Says it all
Of how one Easter morn
My Lord and Savior
Rose from the dead
Conquering all that could
Ever bring me harm

The Blood still fresh
That stains the cross
Says it all
Of how He Bled and Died
Freeing me Forever from the
Bondage of my sin and pride

The Empty Tomb
Says it all
Of His Victory Over Death
The napkin neatly folded
Where once His Head did rest

The scene you see
Says it all
Of the Ultimate Sacrifice
Our Lord and Savior
LOVED US SO HE GAVE US HIS VERY LIFE

But through it all
VICTORY IS OURS
For on that Easter morn
When HE showed those
Nail scarred hands and feet
THE VICTORY WAS ULTIMATELY OURS!

Author: The Father
03-1993

BE WHAT GOD WANTS

Be your own person
To respectfully
Listen and Learn
From those in the past
Who have been burned

To obtain knowledge
From all that you do
And not to allow others
To negatively influence you

To stay focused
And look ahead
Keeping in mind
Life Is your oyster bed

Reminding yourself
Of all you
Can do and it's
TO GOD ALONE
That you must remain true

I WANT TO GO TO HEAVEN

Heaven is a place
Where most want to go
To escape from the agony
Of the earth here below
I want to go to Heaven
Because I know it will be
A Place of Endless Possibilities

Heaven is a place
Where satan was thrown out
Never to return and that's NO DOUBT
I want to go to Heaven
For I know I won't be
Hindered by satan as
I walk Faithfully with My King

Heaven is a place
Where angels have always been
For there they have lived
FREE from all sin
I want to go to Heaven
For there I will be
FREE to Shout, Dance and
WORSHIP MY KING

Heaven is a place
Where we all won't go
Because we have REJECTED JESUS Here Below
I want to YOU to go to Heaven
So ACCEPT HIM TODAY
And you'll get to see JESUS and
HEAVEN is such a Wonderful Place!

2-27-1995

SHOW YOUR LOVE

Love can be expressed
In a variety of ways

Simply by walking
In the park
On a cool spring day
      OR
A sleigh ride
In the winter
On a one horse open sleigh
      OR
A walk on the beach
On a warm summer day
      OR
Just enjoying falling leaves
On a brisk autumn day

Whatever way you show it
It's most that you do
For GOD
Never hesitated
To show HIS LOVE
To YOU

8-6-1996

VISION

Blinded by natural eyes right now I can't see
At least clearly physically
But I see
The deception
The lies
The heartless
As they move

Thinking no one sees them
Because their camouflage
Is so good

But little do they know
That even in the dark
The Eye of the Spirit
Can easily see your heart.

02-07-2010

DO YOU SEE

Do you see what GOD sees
We see a baby lying in a manger
GOD saw HIS SACRIFICE
Our coming KING and SAVIOR

We see the son of a carpenter
Learning his father's skill
GOD saw HIS SON
Working to fulfill HIS Will

We see the miracles
Completed for those who Believed
AND DID COME
GOD saw HIS SON
BUILDING THEIR KINGDOM

We see a miracle worker
Many not sure of who HE is
Riding in on a donkey
Being Hailed as a KING

GOD saw HIS SON
Preparing for HIS
ULTIMATE SACRIFICE
HE would Freely give up HIS Life

We see the Empty Tomb
Symbolizing HE was not there
GOD saw where HE was
JESUS would again be seated

At HIS Father's right hand
The work now COMPLETE!

10-05-2004

FORGIVENESS

Takes a great deal of Vision to see
Because the Empty Cross
Represents forgiveness for you and for me

How is it possible
That this could even be
It's because GOD gave
HIS ONLY SON to set us FREE

HE took our sin and our sickness
And HE was nailed in our place
Because GOD loved us that much
To extent HIS GRACE

HE rose from the tomb
Just ENVISION the SPLENDOR AND Power

GOD knew what HIS children would do
From the beginning
HE had a plan in place from the start
That HE would give us HIS BEST
And Trust us to give HIM our heart

That we would see the plan for us
To fulfill HIS Purpose and
Complete HIS Plan

To be the CREATION
HE designed and
Have Dominion in the PROMISED LAND

10-10-2024

HEALING

Eagles Heal in the Sun

Did you know that when an eagle gets sick it will stretch its wings and fly to the top of a mountain to lie in the sun where it gets healed.? We too, can lay under the SON to be HEALED.

I can personally attest to multiple healings I have experienced. I was told multiple times I should not be here, but God said otherwise. God has shown His healing power many times in my life. While every physical attack was serious, God always brought me through. In March of 2021, my husband took me to the hospital because I had been sick. He told me, "They said you had COVID and I was to take you home and care for you there."

I don't remember any of this happening. My husband did all he could to care for me. However, as time passed, I reportedly stopped eating and was only taking liquid through a turkey baster.

He communicated regularly with our seven children to discuss my progress. My four daughters live in Florida, my three sons in Pittsburgh. Alarmed, the children suggested he take me back to the hospital, which he did not want to do. He insisted he could take care of me like they instructed.

After speaking with her father, my next to the youngest daughter took the helm from Florida. She called an ambulance to come get me. My youngest son came to the house to get their dad. When the ambulance arrived, my son reported to the family that I appeared to be gone. I was informed later that had I been an hour later I would not have survived, my blood pressure had flat lined and my blood sugar was over 600. My daughter ensured that her dad was okay and her mother received the best of care for eight months across state lines.

    I was in a coma for six weeks and had two lung collapses resulting in two ICU stays. I was given medication which created a flesh-eating bacterium on my leg. That bacteria resulted in seven corrective surgeries. Through most of the process, I was not awake. They told my family I might not wake up, I could be brain dead, be put on dialysis, lose my leg, have heart problems or even be a vegetable. My youngest son called me Neo from the Matrix, he said "We quit listening to the doctors."

    As I began to become coherent, I learned about what I had been through. I started physical therapy that lasted several months. God kept me and I learned my new purpose, "to live and not die, but to declare the works of the Lord." Like an eagle, I healed under the watchful eye of the Son.

MENDING A SHATTERED HEART

How do you mend a
SHATTERED HEART
A heart that's been shattered
Into a million tiny pieces
A heart shattered with such force
Many of the pieces have been scattered
NEVER TO BE FOUND
Wounds so deep and an
Such great despair
ONLY a transplant
Could possibly repair

You open your mouth
To let out a scream
But the scream is silent
And no one hears
For it only falls
Upon deaf ears
People too busy
Consumed with themselves
Perception their reality and
They see no one else

IN HIS HANDS

In the Palm of HIS hand
Is where I want to be
A place of total freedom
A place of ultimate safety

In the Palm of HIS hand
That's HIS perfect plan
The place that HE DESIRES
For us ALL to stand

In the Palm of HIS hand
Each name is written clear
To identify that we are
Ultimately HIS

In the Palm of HIS hands
The nail scars from the cross
The evidence of HIS sacrifice
Do bear the LOVE HE gave

For All of us
The Ultimate Sacrifice

8-6-1996

A NEW CREATURE

My transformation from the
Old to the new
Is much like the process
A caterpillar goes through

While wrapped in the cocoon of sin
Nestled so warm and tight within
There was no way out
Until the light of
Jesus Shined In

When the Light of Jesus
Did appear
The process of regeneration
Was put into gear

As I wiggled and struggled
Within in that cocoon
The space was so small
There was no place to move

It was very dark
Within my cramped space
And I could not see
The change that was
Taking Place

I could feel
So much tugging and pain
All over the place
As I was being molded
Right within this
Small space

As Jesus began to peel away
The layered cocoon
I began to emerge
From within my small room

The light shined brighter
As I began to come out
I started to crawl
But then
I found out

The molding and shaping
That had been taking place
Despite so much pain
Had been an act of Grace

For now that darkness
Was no longer there
I was now so
Very keenly aware

Of what our GREAT LORD
Had done for me

Changing and making me
So I could see
The beautiful wings
HE HAD GIVEN ME

Wings of bright color
To fly high in the trees
To view the wondrous
Make of nature and to
Be able to clearly see

The new creature
HE created on the outside
And the inside of me
Was a beautiful Monarch beautiful
HE HAS SET FREE!

DO WE KNOW

We oftentimes don't understand
The pain we must go through

But know that GOD is may not
Feel or see HIM
HE has you in HIS HANDS

Continually working on
HIS PERFECT PLAN
Molding and shaping us

Oftentimes HE'S working as
HE comforts us through
The hearts and care of others
Especially friends like you

TOTAL ACCEPTANCE

Out of all the pain to feel
There is no greater pain
Then the pain that you feel
When you feel your alone
To run this race

When you reach
Out your hand and
It is only
Pushed away

When you express
How you feel and
There is no one there
It seems that hears

The place within yourself
That never seems to
Be filled and
Your many attempts to heal
Seem to produce
No Yield

Yet there is one thing
You should know
Above all in this place

JESUS PAID the PRICE
To provide
ACCEPTANCE IN HIS PLACE

UNDERSTANDING BEING ALONE

Loneliness… the need or desire for someone or something from the outside to fill the void on the inside
Alone…state of being by one's completed self

To know the Joy of
Being Loved
One can Meditate
While All Alone

To Remember the Joy of
A Tender Touch
One Can Feel
While All Alone

But the Wounded Spirit
Feels the heartache of
Not Knowing love and
Longs for the
Tender touch to remember
While All Alone

You don't have to be lonely
While All Alone
For there is someone
Who Can
Bring that tender touch and
Heal Your Broken Heart

He'll share His Love
UNCONDITIONALLY
And if you ACCEPT
HIM in your HEART
HE'S truly Faithful
And from your
Side HE Won't Depart

HIS Name is JESUS
And HE"S there to
Be A Lifelong Friend

12-27-1993

WHY DO WE

Believe in a human
To trust them to do
What ONLY GOD can
To fulfill our desires
And make us complete
To have them to try and meet
Our deep-seated needs

Only to find once again
Do not lean on the arm of a human
For there you will find
Heartache and defeat
And you'll walk away with
Those unmet needs

So while you're lying there
In hurt and defeat
Just look up a little and
HOLD to the MASTER'S feet
For the scars that HE bears
Tells the story so well
Of HIS LOVE for you and me
Which will NEVER FAIL!

Flesh will fail you
That's Guaranteed

GOD has told us
To look to HIM
For ALL of our needs

Yet we continue to go
To the arms of a human
Looking for them to do
What ONLY GOD can

To comfort and love us
To fulfill every need
To bring peace with that
TRUE LOVE AND SECURITY

HEALING

Healing is often a process that GOD guides us through
There is a healing that must take place deep within side of you
ONLY GOD can complete with the willingness of the
Individual and the surrender of bitterness and anger towards
others and most importantly towards oneself.

As I began the road of healing and the process of returning to
Bethel. I trust MY LORD will guide me, lead me, encourage
and strengthen me until I'm in the place with HIM where I
should be.

It is easy to blame others for our inadequacies but much harder
to examine ourselves, realize and accept our part or role in our
own misfortunate or self-destructive behavior

I will always be willing to give the forgiveness that was so freely
given to me and certainly at a GREATER PRICE

We sing "How Great Thou Art" but do we look at the
masterpieces HE has placed ALL AROUND US for our
pleasure. Like the Majesty of the Eagle.

2-12-1993

GOD'S LOVE IS SPECIAL

The love that we have
Is Special
Sent in on the wings
Of a Dove
The love that we have
Is Special
Sealed from OUR LORD
GOD above
The love that we have
Is Special
Wrapped in the warmth of
HIS LOVE
The love that we have
Is Special
Sent from OUR GOD
With LOVE

6-22-1997

I AM A MIRACLE

It's what He called me to be
He infused His spirit deep inside of me
He allowed me to live when satan said I would die.
But God said, "No, you won't, you have no right to her life.
I have work for her to do and she is not finished."

Not even knowing I was taken to the hospital
My family was told I wouldn't live through the night
The King of Kings and Lord of Lords
Sat at the right hand of our Father
Making intercession for me
As they agreed they weren't finished with me

Weeks in a coma just sleeping away
Slowly I began to wake up
No one that I knew did I see
Just machines, doctors and nurses surrounding me

Two lung collapses resulting in ICU stays,
Plus, a flesh-eating bacteria from medication
that tried to eat my leg away
Seven surgeries later to take the bacteria away
I began to awake

As I became more coherent and understood how long I was there
I cried out to my Father and while Thanking Him for being here
I needed to know what my purpose was

He spoke clearly right where I laid
"You will Live and Not Die to declare the works of the Lord"

So just like the story of Job, when all seemed to be taken from Him God continued to stand with him and show him the way through this barren land which he didn't understand

God took me through that land and brought me out on the other side
I can lift my head and hold my hands up high
I can thank the God of the entire world
The only true and living God that spared my life to glorify His.

9-9-2024

PURPOSE

Thunder's Mission

If I Could Be A Flower

Did you know that God has given everyone a purpose?

As I started my life's journey, I thought I knew my purpose. I always planned to be a pediatric doctor. Due to the dysfunction I observed in my family, I didn't plan to get married. Initially, I did not want to have children because I was afraid to lose them. My sister, Yvette, died from SIDS while sleeping in the same bed with me when I was 11 years old.

Those were the plans I made, but I didn't know God. I ended up married and blessed with seven beautiful, healthy children. I knew then that God's purpose for me was not to repeat my family's mistakes. I was to be a wife and mother according to His plan.

Thunder the Eagle

While watching television one night, a program came on about a massive bald eagle that landed in a man's front yard. The man fed the eagle and called animal control for help. They came to secure it and discovered blood-stained dog tags around one of the eagle's talons. They carefully took them off and sent them to be tested once they safely rescued the eagle.

The gentlemen decided to investigate the tags on his own. He checked online and then went to the library looking up the tags and military history. He found details on SKYWATCH and went to a military base to further investigate.

Military personnel told him the eagle's name was "Thunder" and he had been a part of an army training

called "Skywatch." It trained eagles to conduct surveillance in areas that soldiers could not get into. Small cameras were attached to the eagles.
Thunder had been missing in action for several years.

As they began to put things together and track Thunder's path they decided to go out and search the wooded area near the man's house. They found a cabin deep in the woods and contacted authorities. Not only did they find and rescue Thunder's handler who had been wounded, they found another soldier. Both were reunited with their unit and with Thunder.

When I started to wake up from COVID I said to GOD, "I'm grateful for being here and I want to know why you kept me here."

My purpose was clear as God stated to me, "You will live and not die. You will live to declare the works of the Lord."

A DREAMER

My second dad told me
You're a dreamer
That's all you are
And in this life
That won't take you very far

GOD told me
I was a dreamer
And with that
I could succeed
To be everything
I wanted and
ALL HE intended me to be

HE told me
Dreams are the foundation
Of reality
And HE had created
Dreams as a
Integral part of me

HE told me
HE gave me dreams
So I Could
Stretch and Grow
And it was through

HIS DREAMS
The world was created
AND SO

NEVER STOP DREAMING
And continue to be
The Wonderful Creation
GOD has INTENDED
You to be

Call those things that are not as though they were
And you'll see DREAMS become REALITY

8-17-2001

IF I COULD BE A FLOWER

If I could be a
Which one would I be
My Gracious GOD
Has provided
Such a pleasant variety

A TULIP
With long stem extended and
A top to catch the raindrops

A ROSE
Delicate and Beautiful
With a precious scent of Love

Or MAYBE JUST

A WILDFLOWER
Gently blowing in the breeze
Reaching out to touch
GOD'S HAND and
Bowing to HIS KNEE

Whichever I would choose to be
I could be certain of one thing

GOD'S LOVE for me
Would be there
In the midst of everything

BREATHING

Don't let a human be your reason
To exhale

IF they can't provide you
The breath which
You inhale

Don't let someone be your reason
To get up

If they can't give you
The breath to
RISE UP!

12-8-1996

BE WHAT GOD DESIRES

Be your own person
To respectfully
Listen and learn
From those in the past
Who have been burned

To obtain knowledge
From all that you do
And not to allow others
To negatively influence you

To stay focused
And look ahead
Keeping in mind
Life Is your oyster bed

Reminding yourself
Of all you
Can do and it's
To GOD ALONE
That you MUST remain TRUE

FREEDOM

He who the SON
Has set FREE
Is FREE INDEED
TOTALLY FREE

FREE from the chains that bind
FREE from the memories that bring pain

For everything that HE brings
Is Ultimately for OUR gain

Even though the journey
May be through
The Valley of Pain

You will stand on the
Mountain Top
Seeing all the
Ground GOD has BLESSED you to obtain

DON'T LEAN ON THE ARM OF FLESH

You can't trust in dust
For if the wind
Gets in the dust
You don't know
Where or how far
That dust will blow

From dust we came and
To dust we shall return
The dust we return to is made
From OUR FATHER ABOVE

So why would we place our faith and love
In anything but HIS LOVE
ALL the dust that we stand upon
And are made of
Are for HIS special plan

THE CHALLENGE OF LIFE

Life oftentimes appears
To be very unfair
And it will challenge you
If you dare
To look beyond mediocre
To shoot for the moon
As you pass the stars
To embrace the challenge
To know who you are
To be secure
In what GOD has called you to be
Living each day
As it was meant to be!

6-22-1997

FINDING MY WAY HOME

He says He knew me in mother's womb
While not brought up in church
And a Bible I had not read or studied
So I really wasn't clear on the direction
GOD wanted me to go

I played by the rules of the game
Where I thought I could fit in
Little did I know
GOD had a plan for me that had started in the beginning
And it would come to be

I didn't know that just like THUNDER the eagle
GOD had HIS own tracking device on me
HE had a purpose for me to fulfill
A plan where satan would try
To constantly interfere

Through His Divine Plan
And the wonderful instruction drills
God had been preparing me
Much like a Navy Seal
HE sent many people to come my way

They planted, watered and weeded
To keep my enemies away

Even though I wasn't aware of the purpose
Many of the trainings I went through
I learned to stand, pray and fast and war

For the multiple battles I would endure
GOD always brought me out Victorious
And showed me I could accomplish HIS PURPOSE
On land, air or by sea

PRAYING GRANDMA

While living at home
No direction to church or praying did I get
When I started dating my husband
I met someone
Who told me how I could personally talk to
And have a relationship with the
KING OF ALL KINGS
THE GOD OF THE UNIVERSE

She told me to get a bible and read it
And she began to pray for me
Teaching me to stand and walk with the KING.
Through many days and nights
She prayed with me
And prayed me through
Many difficult situations I didn't think I could get through

I miss that praying grandma
For I'm certainly sure
I would not have arrived
To make it through
She was with me by phone
No matter the time of day or night
We read and prayed and sang along
To lift heavy burdens
To continue our travels.

She was someone special and will always Be
Everyone should have such an angel
To guide them on their way.

FORGET YESTERDAY

Each day we can utilize our memories as a tombstone, where you save or as a stepping stone into your future

I am
Where I am

I know
Where I could
Have been
Had I done
What I did not do

Tell me Friend
What I can't
Do today
To be
Where I want to be
 TOMORROW

10-05-2004

AFFIRMATION

The process of growth can be a painful but a necessary one for advancement .

There are always two choices:

1. The pain to gain or
2. The pain to remain the same

The word is a lamp unto my feet and a light unto my path.

Psalm 119:105

HOW GREAT THOU ART

The Earth and ALL of its majesty
Created for HIS GLORY and
To give us pleasure
Certainly tells the story
Nature Alone a Testimony of
    HIS EXISTENCE
No greater art exists or
Has ever been seen
Each season Speaks of
HIS POWER and MAJESTY

SPRING
A time of birth
When everything begins to bloom
A time I always described
As GOD starting HIS painting anew
Splashes of color showing on the landscape
Show through
The grass and trees come forth
With No Help from man

SUMMER
A time when everything
Comes into full bloom
Luscious cascades of flowers
Smelling like the best perfumes
Picnicking in the park

Enjoying the oceans so blue
Even enjoying the nature trails
Exploring the wonders of the world
None of which have been man created
By the hands of man

FALL
The time begins to change
It's harvest time
A range of brilliant colors
On display
Which is reflective of a change
A transformation is in process
That will allow all to rest

WINTER
The well woven tapestry
All a part of HIS PLAN
The temperatures often falling around the world
Some places experiencing snow
Designed to clean the air
The trees now having shed their leaves
In a death like state, they appear to be
Bears hibernate
Some birds migrate some hide away
All of it meant to provide rest
To land and people alike
To rise again when JESUS
Calls it all forth
Saying it was not dead

It was only sleep
And now HIS Life Cycle will
Begin to repeat
      AS HIS
ULTIMATE PLAN IS COMPLETE

10-06-2004

ENTERTAINING ANGELS UNAWARE

We are told in scripture
To beware that we never
    NEVER KNOW
When we entertain angels unaware

At eleven I was introduced
To an Angel
Who was brought
Into My Life
A sister Dawn
Who really brought
Joy and Light
For her very short life

At two months old
Her mission obviously complete
As my angel went home
Lying next to me in her sleep
They said it was SIDS
I would look for hours into the sky
Believing I saw her within the white clouds

GOD then gave me seven angels to live with me
The blessing only a KING could bring
Then the other angels started to arrive
My beautiful grandchildren one by one

All fifteen of them
The first one a granddaughter
She was five generations on both sides of the family
Both maternal and paternal
Our Christine had been a miracle
An angel from above
She touched the lives of many and
Left us far too soon
But in our hearts and memories
She will always be
Because you can NEVER
Forget an Angel or
Their potential possibilities

And looking forward to
Seeing those angels again
As you go before
    OUR KING

ABOUT THE AUTHOR

Sharon Burrell is the Founder and CEO of KINGDOM Service Training & Consulting, LLC. Sharon enjoys helping anyone she can, however she holds a special passion for individuals and their families with autism and mental health diagnosis. She has a sensitivity, compassion, and awareness of the power of effective communication. Sharon believes that dreams can become a reality and that knowledge alone is not power, but knowledge combined with precise action is true power.

Mrs. Burrell has developed a mission to provide counseling for women and minorities. She believes God has a plan and purpose for everyone and through a relationship with Him, His purpose is fulfilled and dreams are fulfilled.

Having completed a dual Ph.D. program (ABD), she offers training and technical assistance to help others start new businesses, successfully operate or expand existing businesses, or develop and make career transitions.

Mrs. Burrell is firm in her belief that without God she could not be or do anything she has done. Sharon has been married to her husband for almost fifty years. Aside from her consulting firm, Sharon operates a business with her husband and they have raised seven children. She is a proud mother to the spouses of her children and a doting grandmother of 15 beautiful grandchildren.

Printed in the USA
CPSIA information can be obtained
at www.ICGtesting.com
CBHW041646121124
17314CB00031B/976